room
crafts

★ American Girl

A big thank you to all our craft testers!

Jordan M., OR
Keeley W., NC
Kat Y., MO
Rene F., NJ
Emily J., TX
Jubilee J., TX
Chelsea S., VA
Tanae S., MN
Abigail K., MI
Natalie M., WI
Madison O., IN
Tina J., IL
Devon G., NY
Petra S., CA
Alyssa H., NJ
Anna R., OH
Rachel R., OH
Megan C., UT
Molly B., MI
Demi P., WA
Alyssa L., WI
Britney B., UT
Sami D., KS
Marissa L., CO
Christine G., MN
Amber M., MI
Danielle D., NJ
Claire S., NJ
Avery M., TX
Lauren C., WA
Carolyn K., MN
Elizabeth H., MN
Kelsey G., MO
Maria H., NY
Foster K., CO
Emily G., MA
Sarah E., PA
Kira M., OR
Cicely W., UT
Jill B., TX
Sarah W., CA
Summer L., IN
Erica M., OR
Ellen M., IL

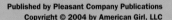

Editorial Development: Sara Hunt, Jessica Hastreiter, Michelle Watkins

Art Direction and Design: Chris Lorette David, Julie Mierkiewicz

Production: Jeannette Bailey, Kendra Pulvermacher, Mindy Rappe, Judith Lary

Photography: Sandy May, Tosca Radigonda, Steven Tailey

Stylists: Tricia Doherty, Jessica Hastreiter, Chris David, Carrie Griffin Boyd, Andrea Ioder, Sena Rosenberg, Cindy Stutzel

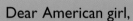

Dear American girl,

If you think your room is **too blah, too baby,** or just plain **too boring,** open this book and open your door to a **new room!**

The crafts in this book offer **simple ways** for you to make **big changes** in your room. You can pick a room theme and do several crafts that coordinate, or browse the pages and pick your favorites. You might choose to do your favorite crafts in one color scheme, or feel free to use our suggested colors as your guide.

When you're done, the most important thing is that you've created something special that adds your **personal touch** to your space.

Your friends at American Girl

table of contents

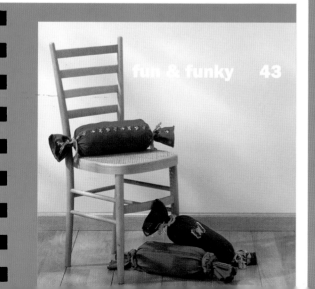

getting started

first things first

If you want to make some changes in your room, first **talk with a parent** to see how much of a change is O.K. with them and how much is too much. What's your budget? Can you paint? Are new sheets and a comforter in your future?

important!

Once you pick a craft to do, **carefully read the instructions all the way through** before you begin. Supplies are marked in **colored type,** so it's simple to make sure you have what you need before you start. If you're changing something major in your

room, like a lamp or furniture, don't forget to ask a parent first!

Always **have an adult help** you with any project where you see this hand 🖐 or when you think something sounds a bit hard for you to do alone.

Cover your work area with newspapers or an old shower curtain when doing messy projects that involve paint or glue. Don't forget to keep craft supplies such as scissors, paint, and beads out of reach of younger siblings.

where to find it

For the items listed, these stores are your best bet, but lots of the materials are available at more than one type of store. Large discount stores with craft, fabric, houseware, and home and office supply sections are a convenient one-stop shopping destination for everything you need.

Craft Store

adhesive-backed felt shapes	elastic thread	paint sponge
confetti wire	embroidery hoop	picture mats
craft glue	fabric paint	pipe cleaners
craft mirror	feather boa	plastic canvas
craft "punch" metal	flat-backed glass stones	pom-poms
decorative ribbon trim	jewel glue	scrapbook paper
double-stick foam tape	memory wire	shadowbox
double-stick tape	mini mirror circles	Tulip® fabric spray paint
earring hooks	Mod Podge®	vellum
	paint pens	wood letters

Fabric Store

appliqués	faux fur	large darning needle
batting	fiberfill	pillow form
	fleece	tulle

Houseware/ Home Design Store

	clip-style picture frame	glass vases
	cork trivet	plastic tray
	cotton jersey pillowcase	

Office Supply Store

adhesive putty	large, flat thumbtacks	transparent 3-ring dividers
CD jewel cases/CDs	metal rim tags	sticky dots
	packing tape	

Hardware/ Home Supply Store

	clothespins	plastic-coated wire
	hooks	yardstick
	picture hangers	

Internet

The Internet is another handy resource for craft supplies and room decor items.

got the green light?

clean your room!

Once you have a parent's permission to make some changes, go through everything in your room and make three piles—keep, toss, and give away.

You can make your room look almost like new simply by getting rid of things you don't want or use anymore. **A clean room is like a fresh start.** Lose the clutter and clear your mind. You might even sleep better if your room is neat and tidy!

organize

After you get rid of the stuff you no longer need, you're ready to get started:

- Get a **bulletin** or **memo board** to keep pictures, papers, and postcards out of a pile and in sight. (Find fun ways to post your papers on pages 19, 30, 38, 47, and 57.)
- Every clean room has a laundry basket and a **wastebasket.** (Ideas to dress up your wastebasket are on pages 15, 26, 38, 44, and 58.)

share, but not alike?

Turn the trouble of having to share your room into the luxury of having double the decorating options! **Mix and match** your sheets to give your beds a makeover. Coordinating, reversible comforters allow you to redecorate daily.

Create **separate rooms** within a room by making a mini wall of bookshelves, hanging a sheet divider from the ceiling, or putting up a store-bought screen that you decorate yourselves.

keep the old

Spend some time "shopping" your house. Sometimes all it takes is a new perspective to make something old new again. For example, try using old suitcases to store out-of-season clothes or collections under your bed. A lamp can make your room feel cozier than the overhead light does. (Personalize your lamp shade with ideas on pages 14, 26, 35, 44, and 54.) A coat of paint can breathe new life into an old wooden chair. If your family is fresh out of old stuff, keep your eye on the curb on trash day. Your neighbor's junk may well be your bedroom's newest treasure! Add a pillow you make yourself (pages 17, 24, 37, 49, and 55), and you've created a new family keepsake.

You don't need expensive artwork to decorate your walls. Add a worldly touch with a colorful map—framed or not. You'll also be surprised how awesome your latest art project looks in a frame on the wall! (For picture-frame decorating ideas, see pages 18, 24, 48, and 55.)

fun shui!

- If you have a TV or computer in your room, **get rid of it!** It zaps the positive "energy" in the room. At the very least, hide electronics in the closet or in a closable desk or armoire.

- Make sure your bed is positioned so you can **see the door.** Also, make sure it's not by a window or against a wall shared with a noisy room—like the bathroom!

- **Blue or green sheets** might be the solution to those sleepless nights because those colors are thought to be calming.

- **A live plant** in your room adds some color and symbolizes growth, life, and well-being. The Chinese especially like live bamboo as a symbol of good luck because it grows really fast.

color your world

Color can dramatically change the look of your room and give it your personal touch. Even if your walls are white, you can add color with a bright bedspread, a cool pillow, or pretty pictures.

- Find a color scheme that **makes you feel good.** Pick one favorite item in your room and build on it. Maybe it's the quilt your dad had when he was little or the pottery you made in art class.

- It's O.K. to pick **your favorite color—**follow your heart! If your favorite clothes are all blue, you'll love how you look in a blue room.

Interior designers suggest picking colors that coordinate.

- **Complementary colors** are colors that are opposite each other on the color wheel, such as **purple** and yellow. **Analogous colors** are next to each other, like **reds** and oranges.

- **Cool colors** like greens, **blues,** and **purples** can make your bedroom feel bigger and neater. **Warm colors** like **reds,** oranges, and yellows can make your room feel cozy and friendly.

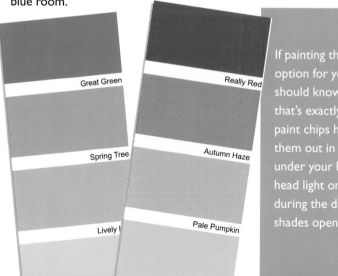

Great Green

Really Red

Spring Tree

Autumn Haze

Lively

Pale Pumpkin

If painting the walls in your room is an option for you, here's something you should know: It can be tricky to find paint that's exactly the shade you want. Bring paint chips home with you and check them out in several different types of light: under your bedside lamp, with the overhead light on and off (both at night and during the day), and with the window shades open in full daylight.

color wheel

Red is bright and bold. While it can be a bit much for your whole room, one or two red walls make a powerful statement.

Orange combines the energy of red with the creativity of yellow. Depending on the shade, orange can make a room feel cozy and warm or soft and delicate.

Purple is a royal color for room decor, but it can be overpowering if the shade is too deep. Look for lilac or lavender to lighten and brighten your lair.

Yellow walls can make you feel sunny and cheerful. Yellow is a great choice for a smart, creative space. Liven up a dark room with bright yellow or make a small room seem bigger with a paler shade of yellow.

Blue is a perfect bedroom color because blue represents peace and quiet. With blue walls in your room, you can't help but feel calm and laid-back.

Green brings the outdoors in and makes your room feel fresh.

warm & fuzzy

snuggle up in your own special spot

lotsa dots

Use **tacky glue** to attach various sizes and colors of **pom-poms** to a small **lamp shade.** Let dry.

fun fur you

Get some fluffy **faux fur** in a hot color. Most faux fur comes in squares. For a small **wastebasket,** use 2 squares. Use **scissors** to trim the fur to fit around the basket. Attach with **tacky glue.** Let dry.

soft light

Flip this fuzzy light switch! Attach **adhesive-backed felt shapes** onto your switch plate.

15

tie it up

Wrap colorful pieces of textured **yarn** around your curtain a few times. Knot on the side, and let the ends hang down.

16

sooo soft

1 Place a square pillow form on a piece of fleece. Cut around the pillow, leaving 4 inches of fleece on each side.

2 Lay the cut piece on top of another piece of fleece in a coordinating color. Cut fleece to the same size with scissors. Place pillow on top in the center. Cut out each corner as shown.

3 Cut an equal number of strips on each side. Strips should be about 4 inches long and approximately 1½ inches wide.

4 Gently lift the top layer of fleece and tuck the pillow between the fleece pieces. Tie fleece strips in double knots around the pillow.

triple frame

1 Tape color copies of **photos** or pictures from magazines to the back of three 8-by-10-inch **picture mats.**

2 Align mats vertically, face down on a table, about 2 inches apart. Use a **ruler** to measure both sides for distance to make sure the mats hang evenly.

3 Fold a 2-yard length of **ribbon** in half. Carefully place ribbon on the mat backs. You can make the top loop as long or short as you like. To center, measure 1¾ inches from the edge of each mat before securing with **high-tack double-stick tape.**

To finish, snip V's in the tail ends of the ribbon with **scissors.**

bloomin' bulletin board

Paint a round **cork trivet** or corkboard with two coats of bright **acrylic paint**. Bend **fuzzy pipe cleaners** to decorate the edges, and secure them on the back with **ultra-tacky** **packing tape** or double-stick tape. Make curlicues by wrapping regular **pipe cleaners** around a **pencil**. Add a stick-on **picture hanger** to the back for easy hanging.

back view

pom-pom pins

Use **tacky glue** to attach **pom-poms** or appliqués to large, flat **thumbtacks**. Let dry.

spell it out

The writing is on the wall! Turn plain **wooden letters** into a colorful message. Mix it up by using different letter styles and by painting each letter a different color of **acrylic paint.** Let dry before hanging. If desired, add stickers and coat with Mod Podge for a fun and fanciful final touch.

tiny table

If you don't have a cool bedside table, make one! Use a **stool** that you already have and put it to work by your bedside. Attach a pretty **ball fringe border** with **double-stick tape** or tacky glue or leave the stool plain and simple. If you don't have a stool, decorate and hang a small shelf at bedside height to get the same table-without-a-table effect!

line up

Wrap **pipe cleaners** around a **vase.** Twist the ends in back to secure. Trim ends with **scissors.** Be careful of the sharp wire ends of the pipe cleaners when twisting them.

bright & light

mark your spot with dots and bright colors

dot-to-dot

Stamp bright circles onto a clean round pillow form with fabric paint and a round paint sponge. To pucker the middle, use a darning needle and yarn to make a few stitches through the center of the pillow. Tie a knot and cut the excess yarn with scissors. Cover the middle with a decoration made from craft foam, plastic or silk flowers, or a combination of them all! Secure with craft glue.

Note: Use the pattern on page 63 and instructions on page 28 to create a perfect plastic flower.

clip pic

Remove the glass from a clip-style picture frame. With fabric puff paint or paint pens, create any pattern or design you like on the surface of the glass (leave room in the middle for your photo). Let dry. Use double-stick tape to attach your photo to a piece of colored paper the size of the frame. If you need to cut the paper to fit, have an adult use your glass piece as a template.

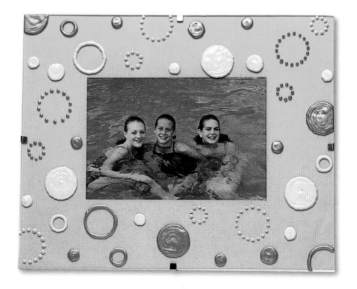

citrus splash

Turn a plain shower curtain into a splashing window cover. First, trim the curtain to the desired length or leave the bottom finished and let it hang to the floor. Next, lay the shower curtain flat on a table. For straight lines, use a yardstick to mark lines with a pencil or erasable pen on the underside, approximately $2\frac{1}{4}$ inches apart. ✌ Have an adult help you cut strips with scissors, stopping about 4 to 5 inches from the top. Mount with matching shower curtain hooks from a standard curtain rod.

Hint: Standard shower curtains are 72 inches by 72 inches. Measure the width of the window you're covering and trim the curtain to fit (use the width from the *outside* edges of the window frame).

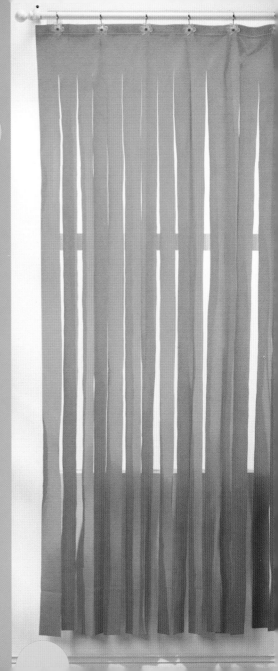

sweet spots

Let dots mark your spot. Use sticky dots
from an office supply store to create a matching
polka-dotted lamp shade and wastebasket.
When you're done, look for other spots you
can decorate with dots!

curtain call

To add a lot of drama for just a little effort, have an adult mount and hang a window
curtain above your bed in place of—or in addition to—a traditional headboard. Use
adhesive hooks on each side of the curtain to hold tiebacks. *Bravo!*

Hint: Use a double rod for a dramatic crisscross curtain.

bright blooms

1 Use the patterns on page 63 to trace flower shapes onto colored plastic 3-ring transparent dividers and two colors of metallic scrapbook paper.

For each flower, make one large and one small shape (any combination). One shape should be plastic, and one paper. 🖐 Have an adult help you cut out the shapes using sharp scissors.

2 Assemble the flowers using double-stick foam tape between the layers. Cut small dots from contrasting scrapbook paper for flower centers. Use double-stick tape to secure in place.

Add life to round flowers by slightly bending forward alternating strips.

3 Attach the back of each flower to a bendable drinking straw with another piece of double-stick tape.

Bend each straw slightly to create a bright and beautiful arrangement of no-fuss flowers!

d. i. y. poster

Why buy a poster like everyone else's when you can make one that's as unique as you are? Use double-stick tape to lightly secure any image you choose—a pattern cut from wrapping paper or wallpaper scraps, or even your own artwork—onto brightly colored poster board. Secure into an inexpensive poster frame. You're done!

mini memo minder

Have an adult help you remove and set aside the glass from an 8-by-10-inch picture frame. If the frame is wood, paint it with acrylic paint, if desired. Let dry.

Have an adult help you insert an 8-by-10-inch sheet of magnetic craft, or "punch," metal into the picture frame. Replace frame back.

memo magnets

Paint a few small wood shapes with acrylic paint. Let dry. Attach a small magnet to the back of each shape with craft glue. For sparkly circles, brush colored round magnets with craft glue. Sprinkle with glitter. Let dry.

31

cool & casual

create a hangout where you can chill out

hold it

Use **scissors** to cut 2-foot-
long pieces of 8-inch-wide
tulle in various colors. Wrap
tulle strands around a curtain
and tie. String on **pony beads**
for added sparkle.

great graphic

Cut squares of **tissue paper** with **scissors**.
Cover a small area of a **glass vase** with **Mod
Podge** using a **sponge brush** or paintbrush.
Attach tissue paper squares. Repeat until the
whole vase is covered. Finish by applying a coat
of Mod Podge over the entire vase. Let dry.

made in the shade

Cut an 8½-by-11-inch sheet of **vellum paper** into 2-inch strips with **scissors**. (If you have a big shade, you will need 2 pieces of paper.) Put **double-stick tape** on the top edge of the **lamp shade** and on the end of each vellum strip. Press tape to the top of the shade. Cut the remaining ends of vellum so that they hang slightly over the bottom edge of the shade.

decoupage collage

Cover a small area of a **plastic tray** with **Mod Podge**, using a **sponge brush** or paint-brush. Attach cutouts from **tissue paper, stationery, and textured specialty paper.** Repeat until the whole tray is covered. Finish by applying a coat of Mod Podge over the entire tray. Let dry.

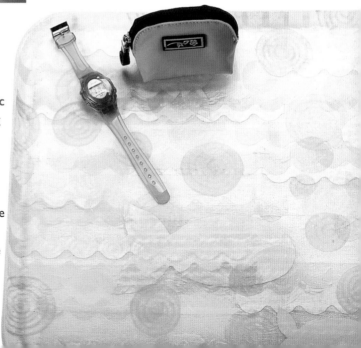

dream on!

Keep bad dreams out of your room with your own hand-made dream catcher.

1 Cut a piece of thin **memory wire** so that it makes a 5-inch circle. String **seed beads** onto the wire, leaving space at the end for a jewelry **crimp bead.** Use the crimp bead to close the circle.

2 Knot a long piece of **jewelry cord** onto the wire. Crisscross the cord back and forth across the circle, creating a web. If desired, add a light-weight **bead** occasionally. Tie a knot and trim the excess.

3 Add a bead to a length of jewelry cord and make a knot below the bead. Tie the cord to the bottom of the circle. Repeat for 2 additional lengths. Make a loop of jewelry cord or thread at the top for hanging.

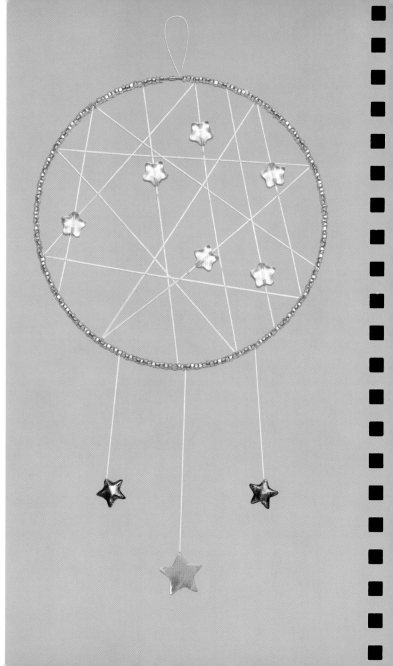

so simple

Find a **large patterned bandanna** or a
square of cotton fabric. Place a small **throw
pillow** diagonally on the fabric. Wrap the fabric
around the pillow and knot opposite corners
of the square in back.

wiggle wire

Wire your walls with a wiggly place to clip pictures and notes. Curl a desired length of **plastic-coated electrical wire** (test it to make sure it bends and holds its shape). Make a small loop on each end to hang from nails or hooks on your wall.

mix & match

Rip pieces of pretty **patterned paper.** Cover portions of a **wastebasket** with **Mod Podge,** using a **sponge brush.** Attach paper pieces, overlapping the edges. Finish with a coat of Mod Podge over the paper. Let dry. Attach **flat-backed glass stones** with **jewel glue.** Let dry.

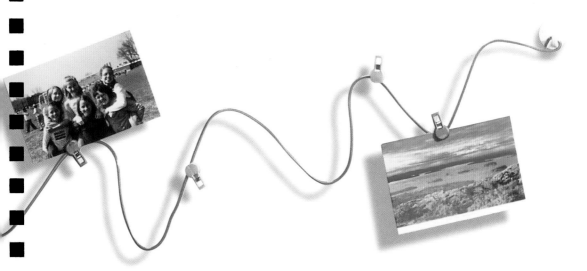

shadowbox

Create a keepsake box to highlight vacation memories or a special hobby. Start by painting a **shadowbox** with **acrylic paint.** Let your imagination take it from there.

To bring the background to life, try **mosaic craft-glass pieces** or **scrapbook paper.** Glue a decorative **magnet** inside, or tape a special **bracelet** or key chain to the top of the box. For a 3-D effect, mount photos with thick **foam mounting tape.**

Use reusable **adhesive putty** to prop up trinkets, souvenirs, or photos.

Decorate the frame by gluing to the edge some **small magnetic words** or words cut from magazines, or glue **letter beads** to the front of the box. Use **stickers** to decorate the sides of the box.

bed headboard

1 Cut a piece of **heavy cardboard** as wide as your bed, and about 30 inches high. If the cardboard isn't very heavy, **tape** 2 pieces together.

2 Cut a piece of thick **batting** the same size as the cardboard. Place it on top and tape each edge down loosely.

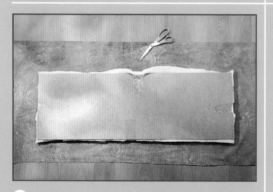

3 Lay **fabric** on the floor, right side down. Put batting and cardboard on top of it, with the batting against the fabric. (If fabric has a design, make sure it's centered under the batting.) Cut the fabric about 6 inches larger than the cardboard all the way around.

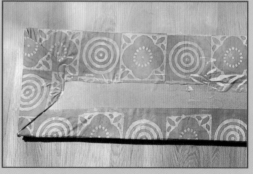

4 Fold the fabric all around the cardboard and batting (like you were wrapping a present), and use **packing tape** to secure the edges.

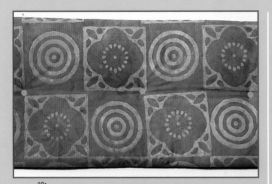

5  Have an adult help you hold the head-board against the wall above your bed and **nail** it in 3 places to the wall to secure.

6 Cover nail heads by gluing big **buttons** or appliqués over them.

Note to adult: For best results, be sure at least one of the nails hits a wall stud.

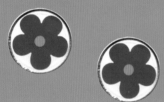

fun & funky

reuse simple stuff to redo your room

bead basket

Add some class to your trash! Use double-stick tape to attach colorful beaded ribbon trim to the top and bottom of a wicker wastebasket.

beadazzled lamp

Thread 8 earring hooks with elastic thread. Tie a knot on each and add beads to desired length. Finish with another knot. Trim excess thread with scissors. Hook beaded strings evenly around the outside of a lamp shade.

tag!

Your room will be "It!" when you turn metal rim tags into these cool curtains. Simply use colored highlighters or markers to color several strung metal rim tags. Decorate others with pretty stickers.

Punch a hole in the bottom of each tag with a hole punch. Use slip knots to string the tags together (see instructions below). Trim excess string with scissors. Repeat until you've reached the desired length (about 12 tags per strand). Make as many—or as few—strands as you like. Loop each strand over a curtain rod with a slip knot, or tape it to the wall or the frame above your window.

Hint: To make a slip knot, thread the doubled string from one tag (leave the knot intact) through the hole in another. Open the thread to make a loop, and pull the tag through.

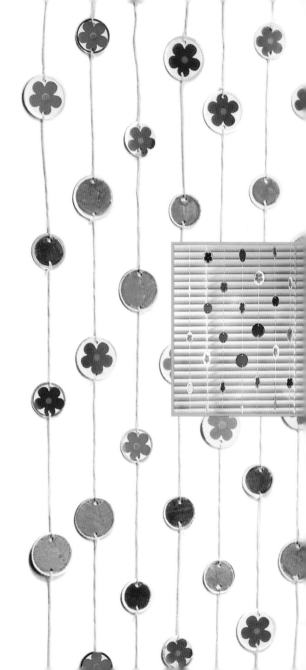

bright bottles

Wash and rinse empty glass soda bottles, such as IBC or Stewart's. Shake out excess water and allow to air dry. Fill bottles with about 4 tablespoons acrylic paint, then pour excess paint back into its container. Lay bottles on their sides and rotate once every 5 minutes for about an hour. Let dry upside down over an empty can overnight. Let dry completely for several days before adding contents.

yardstick clipboard

To create this clever clipboard, paint a yardstick and several wood clothespins. Let dry. Glue appliqués or other decorations onto the clothespins (if desired). Let dry. Hang the clipboard from a nail on your wall. It rules!

bottle cap mirror

Glue twist-off soda bottle caps around the border of a plain craft mirror. Let dry. Top off each cap with a sticker inside. Use ultra-tacky packing tape to attach a ribbon to the back for hanging.

47

funky frames

Turn CD jewel cases into fun frames. Carefully remove the center piece from the case and set aside the back jacket. Tape a picture inside the CD case, facing out. Decorate the outside of the case with craft glue and fabric trim, ribbon, beads, buttons, or stickers. Let dry.

Note: Depending on the type of CD case you have, you can position the CD case so that it sits open for two side-by-side pictures, stands upright like an easel, or flips back to rest open with one photo displayed.

back blues

This pillow fits like your favorite pair of jeans! First, cut one leg off an old pair of tights. Stuff the leg snugly with fiberfill stuffing to make a tube about 12 inches long. Next, cut the leg off an old pair of jeans (ask first!), making a piece about 18 inches long. If you like, cut both ends so that the edges will fray in time like your favorite pair of cutoffs. Center the tights tube inside the jeans leg. Secure the ends with hair elastics or yarn.

untie-dye pillowcase

1 Wash and dry a white 100% cotton jersey knit pillowcase. Do not use fabric softener. Cover your work area with trash bags or newspapers.

2 Line the pillowcase with a tall kitchen garbage bag and lay it flat on your work surface. Spray pillowcase with water to dampen slightly.

3 Use a variety of colors of spray-on fabric paint to mimic real tie-dye patterns right onto the surface of your pillowcase. For ripples or crackles, scrunch or fold fabric before spraying. Spray more or less, closer or farther away to achieve desired color and intensity. Spray a small area at a time, allowing paint to overlap and blend for a "tie-dye" look.

4 Let the pillowcase dry 24 hours. Repeat painting on reverse side. Wait at least 72 hours before washing in mild detergent. Line dry.

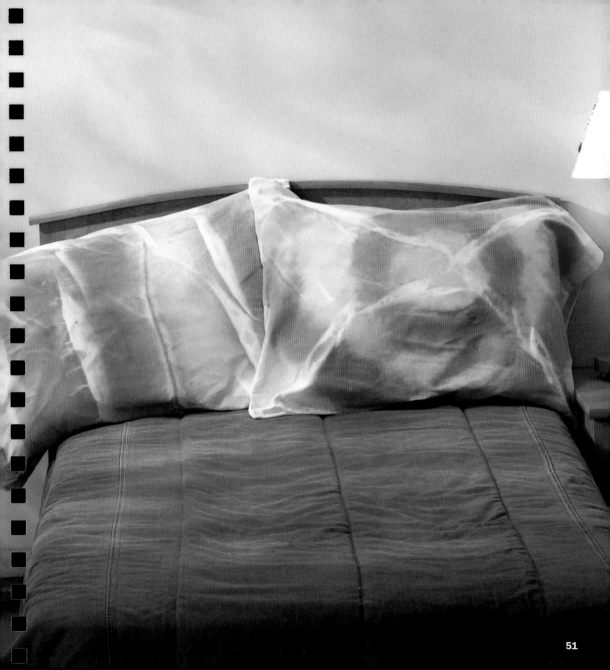

51

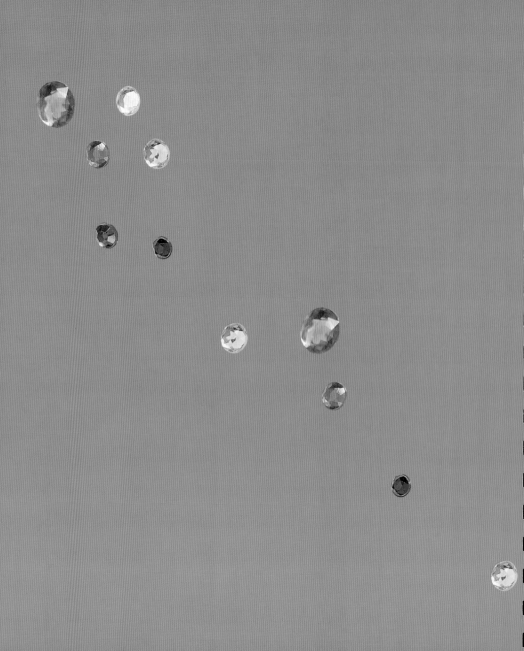

hip & happenin'

you'll shine in this sparkly suite

glamour glow

Use **jewel glue** to attach **rhinestones** and
mini mirror circles to a **lamp shade.** Let dry.
String sparkly **beads** on a glittery **pipe cleaner**
and wrap it around the base of the lamp.

pillow poof

Cut 2 pieces of colorful, shiny **fabric** long enough to wrap around a small **throw pillow.** Wrap one piece around the pillow and tie the ends. Repeat with the other piece. Wrap a **hair elastic** around all loose ends so that they stand up.

glittery gal

Use **jewel glue** to attach **craft jewels** or mini mirror circles to an **acrylic picture frame.** Let dry.

sun sparkler

Catch a rainbow of light with recycled **CDs**.
Glue a piece of **fishing line** between 2 old
CDs so that the plain silver sides face out.
Decorate both sides with glittery **fabric paint**
and a few **rhinestones.** Let dry, and then hang
in a sunny window to catch some rays.

fluffy stuff

Change your bulletin board from dreary to cheery! Paint the cork with **acrylic paint.** Let dry. Use **craft glue** to attach a **feather boa** to the frame. Let dry.

flashy tacks

Make your point with these neat glass tacks! Paint simple designs on the backs of **flat-backed glass stones** with **acrylic paint.** Let dry. Use **tacky glue** to attach the stones onto large, flat **thumbtacks.**

boa trim

Trim a **feather boa** to fit around the top edge of a **wastebasket**. Wrap the boa around the basket and secure with a **binder clip**.

sparkle vase

Press **glitter stickers** onto a clear **vase**. Use **jewel glue** to attach **rhinestones**. Let dry. (You can even find stickers that have rhinestones on them!)

star swirl

Wrap colorful **confetti wire** around your curtains to tie them back.

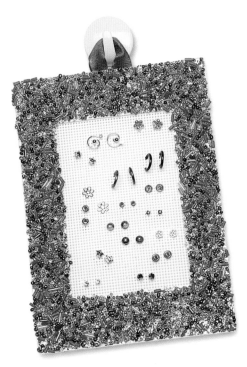

pair care

Trim a piece of **plastic canvas** to fit on the back of a **picture mat. Glue** the canvas to the back. Let dry. Apply **double-stick tape** to the front of the mat and place it in an empty shoe box. Sprinkle on **seed beads, bugle beads,** and **microbeads.** Press until the beads stick. **Tape** on a **ribbon** and hang it up!

dreamy drape

1 Separate a plastic 12-inch adjustable **embroidery hoop**. Cut 4 pieces of **ribbon,** 24 inches each. Tie one end of each ribbon to the larger hoop. Gather the other ribbon ends at the top and tie them in a knot.

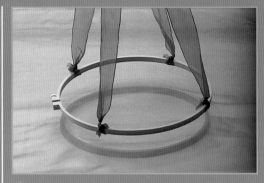

2 Center the smaller hoop underneath the middle of 5 yards of 45-inch-wide **tulle** or netting. Press the larger hoop on top, sandwiching the fabric and ribbon. Tighten the hoop.

3 Ask an adult to screw a **ceiling hook** into the ceiling above the head of your bed. Hang the canopy on the hook.

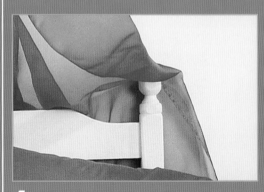

4 Loop the fabric over your headboard or secure with additional pieces of ribbon. If you don't have a headboard, you can attach hooks to the wall for tiebacks.

STARS

shining stars

Jazz up your reflection with **starry garlands** and sparkly **stickers**. Keep **dry-erase markers** handy and get your mirror autographed by all the stars who visit your dressing room!

Mindy

Chris

Cassie

patterns

Request a FREE catalogue!

Books are just the beginning...

Discover dolls, clothing, furniture, and accessories that inspire girls to imagine their own stories.

Just mail this card, call 1-800-845-0005, or visit americangirl.com.

Girl's name _____ Girl's birth date ___/___/___

Address _____

City _____ State _____ Zip _____

Parent's e-mail *(for order information, updates, and Web-exclusive offers)*

( ) _____
Parent's phone _____ ❑ Home ❑ Work

Parent's signature _____ 12583i

Send a catalogue to a grandparent or a friend:

Name _____

Address _____

City _____ State _____ Zip _____

❑ Grandparent 15262li   ❑ Friend 12591li

B2732

Try it risk-free!
Simply mail this card today!

16 **Crafts** for Your Room

Slumber Party **Snacks!**

Advice for Dealing with Jealousy

The magazine especially for girls 8 and up!

Mail this card to receive a **risk-free** preview issue and start your one-year subscription. For just $22.95, you'll receive 6 bimonthly issues! If you don't love *American Girl* right away, just write "cancel" on your invoice. The preview issue is yours to keep, free!

❑ 1 year (6 issues) $22.95

Send bill to: (please print)

Adult's name _____

Address _____

City _____ State _____ Zip _____

Adult's signature _____

M4626

Send magazine to: (please print)

Girl's name _____ Birth date *(optional)* _____

Address _____

City _____ State _____ Zip _____

Guarantee: You may cancel at any time for a full refund. Allow 4–6 weeks for first issue.
Non-U.S. subscriptions $29 U.S., prepaid only. © 2006 American Girl, LLC.

K71AGL

Visit americangirl.com
and click on **Fun for Girls**
for quizzes and games.

PO BOX 620497
MIDDLETON WI 53562-0497

BUSINESS REPLY MAIL
FIRST-CLASS MAIL   PERMIT NO. 190   BOONE IA

POSTAGE WILL BE PAID BY ADDRESSEE

Magazine Subscription Dept.
PO BOX 5532
HARLAN IA 51593-3032

Look for these and other bestselling books from American Girl:

American Girl celebrates a girl's inner star—that little whisper inside that encourages her to stand tall, reach high, and dream big. We take pride and care in helping girls become their very best today, so they'll grow up to be the women who make a difference tomorrow.

8+ 59113 $9.95

Printed in China

ISBN 1-58485-911-3

50995
9 781584 859116